7-11

D1417554

My World

THE WEATHER

By Gladys Rosa-Mendoza • Illustrations by C.D. Hullinger

WINDMILL BOOKS
New York

Published in 2011 by Windmill Books, LLC
303 Park Avenue South, Suite # 1280, New York, NY 10010-3657

Adaptations to North American Edition © 2011 Windmill Books, LLC
First published by me+mi publishing, inc. © 2007
Text and illustrations copyright © me+mi publishing, inc., 2007

CREDITS:
Author: Gladys Rosa-Mendoza
Illustrator: C.D. Hullinger

Library of Congress Cataloging-in-Publication Data

Rosa-Mendoza, Gladys.
  The weather / by Gladys Rosa-Mendoza ; illustrated by CD Hullinger. — School & Library Edition
      p. cm. — (My world)
  Originally published: Wheaton, Ill. : Me+mi Pub., 2000.
  Includes index.
  ISBN 978-1-60754-955-0 (library binding) — ISBN 978-1-61533-043-0 (pbk.) — ISBN 978-1-61533-044-7 (6-pack)
  1. Weather—Juvenile literature. I. Hullinger, C. D., ill. II. Title.
  QC981.3.R648 2011
  551.5—dc22
                                2009054430

Manufactured in the United States of America

For more great fiction and nonfiction, go to www.windmillbooks.com

CPSIA Compliance Information: Batch #S10W: For further information contact Windmill Books, New York, New York at 1-866-478-0556.

Contents

What's the weather?
Today it's sunny.

That's good weather
for a soccer game.

Taylor is about to kick the ball.

Today it's raining.

6

Sarah has her raincoat
and umbrella.

Her raincoat is orange.

It is fun to fly a kite
on a windy day.

The wind can also
blow off your hat!

When there is a storm everyone wants to stay inside the house.

The Russo family is sitting in their house on the couch.

They are watching the
storm outside.

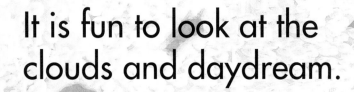

It is fun to look at the
clouds and daydream.

Zach and Hannah are talking about the shapes they see in the clouds.

It snows in the winter.

It is fun to build snowmen
when it snows.

The kids have built a
big snowman!

Look at all the beautiful colors in the rainbow!

Can you name all of the colors in this rainbow?

There are four seasons.

spring

fall

They are spring, summer,
fall, and winter.

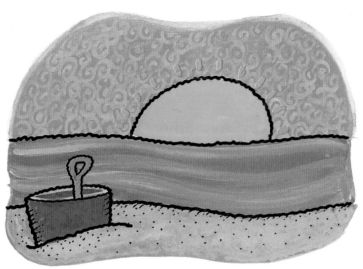

summer

 winter

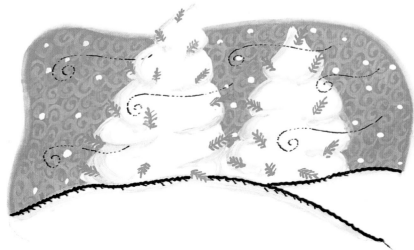

Read More!

Nonfiction

Eckart, Edana. *Watching the Weather.* Danbury, CT: Children's Press, 2004.

Harris, Caroline. *Weather.* New York: Kingfisher, 2009.

Fiction

Bauer, Marion Dane. *If Frogs Made the Weather.* New York, Holiday House, 2005.

Holub, Joan. *Groundhog Weather School.* New York: Putnam Juvenile, 2009.

Learn More!

 Rain clouds look darker than other clouds. They look darker because they are full of water.

 The world's biggest snowman was built in 2008 in Maine.

 If the light is right, you can sometimes see two or even three rainbows at once.

Take a look outside. What is the weather like today? Can you guess what the weather will be like tomorrow?

Words to Know

clouds (klowds) masses of water vapor in the sky

fall (fahl) the season after summer and before winter when leaves fall from the trees

rain (rayn) drops of water that fall from the sky

rainbow (RAYN-bohw) band of colors in the sky

snow (snohw) frozen drops of water that fall from the sky when it is cold outside

spring (spring) the season after winter and before summer

storm (stohrm) heavy rain with thunder and lightning

weather (WEH-thur) how warm or cold it is, or if it is raining or snowing

summer (SUH-mur) the season between spring and fall

wind (wihnd) the movement of air

umbrella (um-BREH-la) a covering that can protect you from the rain

winter (WIN-tur) the season between fall and spring when it is cold outside

23

Index

Web Sites

For Web resources related to the subject of this book, go to:
www.windmillbooks.com/weblinks and select this book's title